The Rubbish Robot

Written by
Cath Jones

Illustrated by
Tom Heard

Michelle was an inventor.

She was good at inventing things, but she was quite untidy too. Her workshop was always a mess, because she never put anything away.

There were dirty plates sitting on the bench and piles of rubbish on her desk. There was even some mould growing on a pair of stinky old socks!

Michelle's mum was not happy about the mess.

"You know the rules," she said. "You need to tidy up, now."

But Michelle had invented a robot to clear up the mess for her. She gazed at it proudly.

"I will call you the Rubbish Robot," she said, "because I made you to clear up rubbish."

When she pressed the start button, the robot sucked and scrubbed and polished.

Soon, Michelle's workshop was glistening!

When Mum came in, she didn't see the robot. She thought Michelle had cleared up the mess.

"This is fantastic, Michelle," she said. "Well done!"

From then on, every night when Michelle went to bed, the Rubbish Robot set to work. For the whole night it sucked and scrubbed and polished.

Then, one day, the Rubbish Robot started to malfunction. It no longer sucked and scrubbed and polished.

Michelle checked the sucker. It was bunged up with dirt. The robot's body looked very grubby too.

"I think you need a wash," she said.

She popped the Rubbish Robot into the bath and turned on the taps.

She rubbed on some soap, tipped up the shampoo and lathered up her robot.

This will fix it, she thought.

The next time Michelle pressed the start button, there was a **CLUNK! BLIP! POP!**

The robot sucked up all the rubbish, but then it sprayed it all back out again! It blew everywhere!

Then the robot started to travel in the wrong direction. Now it was blowing rubbish all over the house!

Michelle pulled the special emergency stop cord. Instantly the robot stopped blowing out rubbish.

She looked around at the mess. Oh dear! The whole house was a wreck.

When Mum came home, she looked around at the mess.

"What is going on?" she asked.

Michelle told her about the Rubbish Robot.

"You invented a robot!" Mum said. "What a clever inventor you are! But now it's broken, you'd better start clearing up the mess."

Michelle scrubbed and polished all day long. At last, the house was clean and tidy.

When she got into bed, she fell into a deep sleep.

While she slept, she had lots of dreams.

When she woke up, she knew just what to do.

Michelle invented a machine to wash her Rubbish Robot. This time, she was sure that nothing could go wrong!